1. Aileron
2. King post wing bracing
3. Aileron horn (or pylon)
4. Upper plane or wing
5. Leading edge
6. Aileron control wire
7. Trailing edge
8. Upper drag wire
9. Strut (spruce)
10. Exhaust stacks
11. Engine cowl
12. OX-5 V-8 engine
13. Engine hood fix straps (leather)
14. Propeller
15. Propeller hub
16. Tip shields (copper)
17. Radiator
18. Motor bed (laminated ash and spruce)
19. Fuel tank
20. Access door to carburetor and crankcase oil drainplug

21. Lower drag wire
22. Landing gear struts
23. Seizing (linen cord)
24. Wing tip skid
25. Tether ring
26. Lower plane
27. Mounting step
28. Aileron control quadrant
29. Front (observer's) cockpit
30. Dual controls
31. Front instrument panel
32. Fuel gauge
33. Fuel shutoff
34. Rear instrument panel
35. Throttle control
36. Rear (pilot's) cockpit
37. Cockpit padding
38. Seat (woven wicker) and seat belt
39. Elevator cable walking beams
40. Truss post (spruce)
41. Turnbuckle
42. Cable truss (stranded steel)
43. Longerons (spruce and ash)
44. Cowling (aluminum)
45. Turtleback fairing
46. Fuselage
47. Fairleads (leather)
48. Rudder cables
49. Fabric covering (doped cotton or Irish linen)
50. Tail skid
51. Tail skid shock absorber (rubber cord)
52. Tail skid shoe (steel)
53. Brace (steel tube)
54. Elevator control cables
55. Horizontal stabilizer
56. Vertical stabilizer
57. Rudder
58. Elevator horns
59. Pinked tape
60. Guy lines
61. Elevator

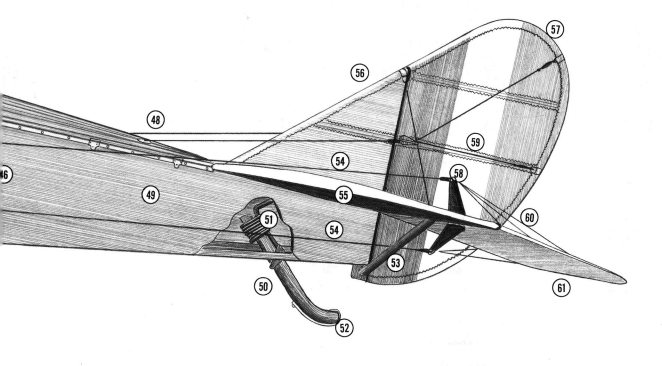

# JENNY

## *The Airplane That Taught America to Fly*

DAVID WEITZMAN

ROARING BROOK PRESS

Brookfield, Connecticut

For Tom Lawrence

Published by Roaring Brook Press
A division of The Millbrook Press, 2 Old New Milford Road, Brookfield, Connecticut 06804

Library of Congress Cataloging-in-Publication Data
Weitzman, David.
Jenny : the airplane that taught America to fly / David Weitzman.—1st ed.
     p.    cm.
Summary: Presents the development and history of the JN-4D airplane, commonly called the Jenny,
and portrays a typlical woman pilot who trained army air cadets for World War I and later carried air mail.
1. JN-4D (Training plane)—History—Juvenile literature. 2. Aeronautics—United States—History—Juvenile
literature. [1. JN-4D (Training plane)—History. 2. Airplanes—Design and construction. 3. Women air pilots.
4. Aeronatics—History.] I. Title.
TL686.C8 W45 2002
629.133'343—dc21     2002069709

ISBN 0-7613-1547-0 (trade edition)
10 9 8 7 6 5 4 3 2 1
ISBN 0-7613-2565-4 (library binding)
10 9 8 7 6 5 4 3 2 1

Manufactured in China
First Edition

**O**ne cold and rainy afternoon, while rummaging in the attic of their grandmother's house in upstate New York, the children discovered a model airplane and an album bulging with old photographs. They brought their treasures to their grandmother and asked her about the pictures of the woman with the airplane.

*Mom*

and Her Jenny

Oh my, it's been a long time since I've seen these. They are pictures of my mother, your great-grandmother. And that airplane is her Jenny. She was one of the first women in America to get a pilot's license. In 1914, she trained Army air cadets for the First World War—she wanted to fly combat missions, but they wouldn't let her. Then, after the war ended, she carried air mail.

Mom always talked about her Jenny with real love—the airplane's official name was JN4-D, but everyone called them Jenny. Thousands were built during the war, more than anyone thought possible. And when it was over, the manufacturer, Glenn Curtiss, bought them back from the Army and put them up for sale. Jennys became the favorite of barnstormers, those daredevil pilots who flew around the country and put on shows. The first airplane I ever saw was a Jenny flown by a barnstormer, and that was true for most Americans. They did wing walking and all kinds of crazy stunts. In one of the photographs, there's a man sitting out by the tail. And when the show was over, they'd take people up for rides.

Mom said it was easy to learn. She flew three hours with an instructor, touching down and lifting off maybe ten times. That was all! After just a few more hours of practice, she made her first cross-country flight. Of course, they made short hops in those days. Jenny's gas tank held just enough for about two hours of flying, and then you had to find place to land. An "airport" was usually just a pasture. You would fly low over it a few times to make sure the grass wasn't too high, that there were no ditches or tall brush which could catch your landing gear and flip the plane over.

When my mom was little like you, there were very few people in the whole world who had ever flown. Then Mr. Curtiss came along and made a lot of airplanes and set up flying schools. America learned to fly in Mr. Curtiss's airplanes. Just about every pilot in America and England between the wars learned to fly in a Jenny, including Amelia Earhart and Charles Lindbergh. And upstate New York, where the Jennys were built, became known as "the cradle of aviation."

The June Bug was one of Glenn Curtiss's first aeroplanes—that's what they called them in those days, aeroplanes. Its frame was made of bamboo, a strong, hard wood, a common material for airplane frames. Glenn Curtiss told the story that when he was a boy he attached a sail to a bamboo fishing pole, held it up into the wind, and sailed across the frozen lake on his ice skates.

The wings, or planes as they were called then, were at first covered with plain cotton muslin or linen. But if the airplane got caught in the rain or snow, the cloth absorbed water, adding as much as fifty pounds to its weight and causing a lot of crashes. So builders began coating the cloth with "wing dope," a mixture of turpentine, paraffin, and gasoline. Yellow ochre pigment was also added to the dope, making the airplane bright yellow.

The June Bug was one of the first airplanes to have wheels. The Wright brothers believed that flying machines could only take off from tracks. But Glenn Curtiss had a lot of experience with wheels. If those spoked wheels on the June Bug and the Jenny look familiar to you, it's because, before he built airplanes, Mr. Curtiss built bicycles and motorcycles. He once built a V-8 engine, mounted it on a motorcycle, and reached 136.3 miles per hour. In 1907 that was the fastest any vehicle had ever gone, and Curtiss was known as "the fastest man on Earth."

Mr. Curtiss's first airplanes were called "pushers," because the engine and propeller pointed backwards, pushing the airplane through the air. That's the way the June Bug flew. And that's the way Orville and Wilbur Wright built their first airplanes. The other kind of airplane is called a "tractor," more like we're used to seeing, with the engine and propeller up front pulling the plane through the air.

Mr. Curtiss preferred pushers because the pilot could sit right up in front and see in every direction. People who liked tractors joked that the problem with pushers was that you had to look behind you all the time to see if the airplane was coming or not!

There was one problem with having the engine up front. The cylinder heads on Jenny's engine stuck out to keep them cooler, but the oil lubricating the valves would end up all over the pilot. I remember Mom telling me how she'd be constantly flying in a mist of castor oil that coated her face and goggles. Years later she said she could still taste that nasty stuff.

Eventually Curtiss had to give up his pusher idea. Tractor aircraft were proving to be better performers—and safer. The Army, for whom Curtiss was training pilots at his flying schools, had announced they were changing over from pushers to tractors. So he began thinking about building one himself.

In 1913, while he was traveling in England, Curtiss met an engineer, B. Douglas Thomas, who had already begun making sketches and calculations for a tractor biplane. Curtiss invited him to come to his shop in Hammondsport, New York, with the idea that they would each design an airplane and manufacture the best one. Thomas completed his plans for a J model, which flew over eighty-five miles per hour, making it the fastest airplane manufactured in the United States. Curtiss, meanwhile, had designed an N model. They combined the best features of the J and the N and came up with the JN. Jenny proved to be a perfect trainer. She was easy to fly and very stable.

The next year our little town was suddenly caught up in a faraway war. It soon became clear that this war—the First World War—would be fought in the air as well as on the ground. And, who would have guessed that Hammondsport would become so important? The British Army told Glenn Curtiss that they wanted him "to build all the planes you can, as fast as you can."

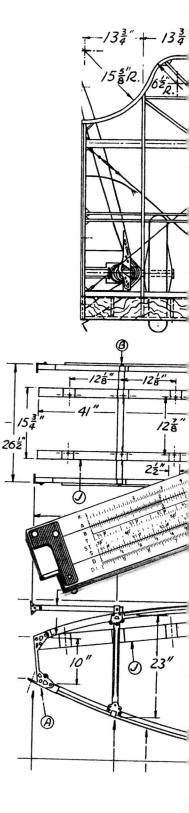

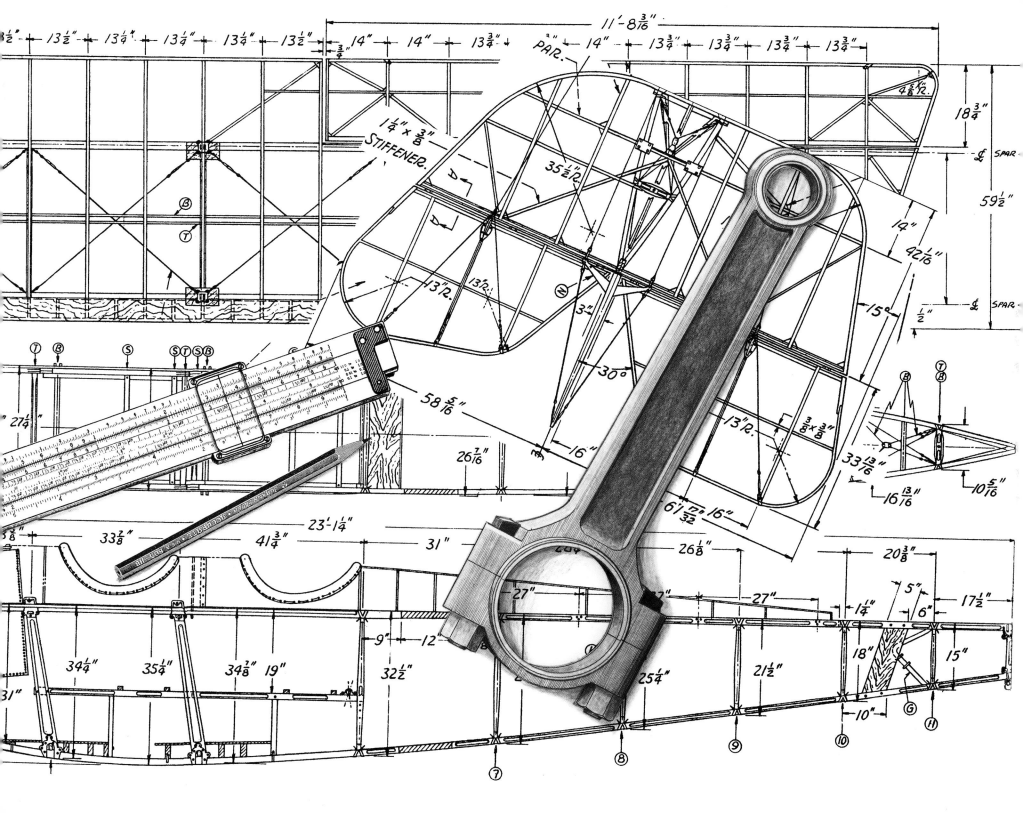

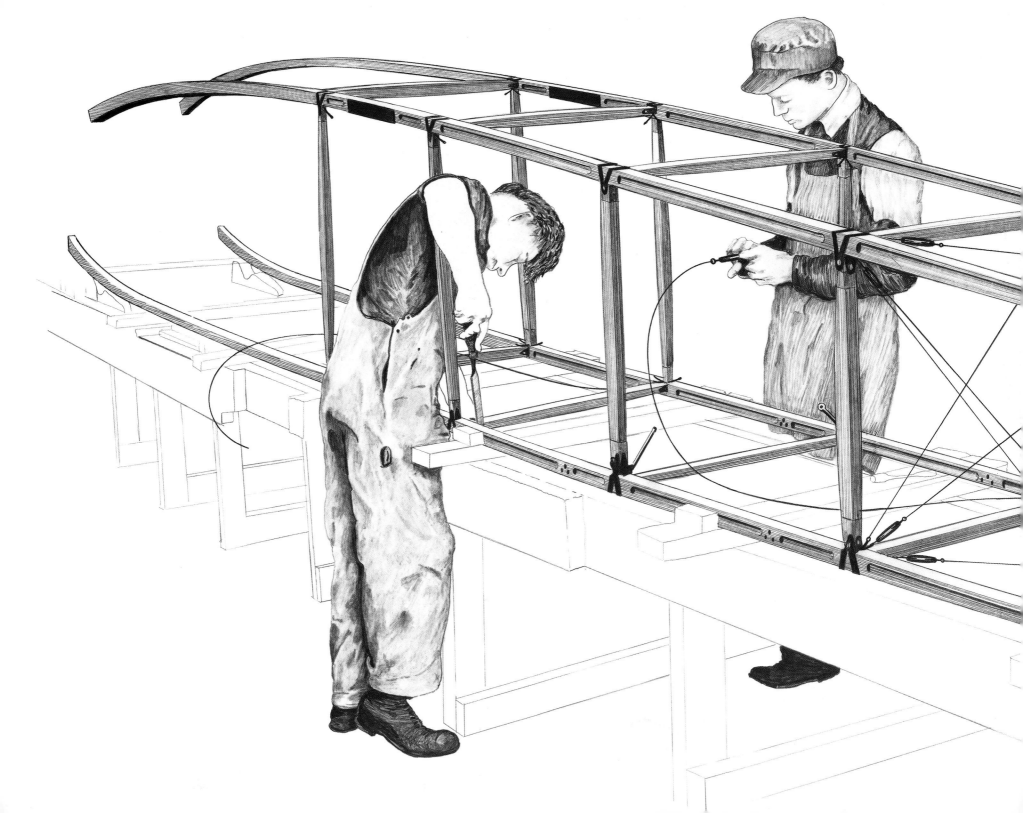

The Jenny was already in production. Each was made of carefully chosen sticks of spruce, ash, birch, and pine dried in kilns. These woods are so strong that frame members like the longerons (the long, horizontal sticks) only needed to be 1 1/2 inches by 1 1/4 inches thick. The frame was fitted and fastened together by hand, glued, and then varnished like a fine cabinet. Wire cables, stretched diagonally in all directions and tightened with turnbuckles, tied the longerons and struts (vertical sticks) together into a rigid box that could resist the jolts, stresses, and vibrations of flight.

The Jenny had quite a wingspan. The upper wing was over forty-four feet long, and the lower almost thirty-four feet from tip to tip.

The long, heavy pieces, called spars, tied together all the compression ribs that gave the wing its shape—curved on top, flat on the bottom. The ribs were sawn out of plywood and holes were cut to reduce weight. Each wing panel could easily be lifted and moved around by two people.

The workers would screw down a thin plywood covering on the leading edge of the wing with a marvelous tool called a Yankee drill and screwdriver. Just by moving the handle up and down they could quickly drill a hole or, with the screwdriver tip, set a screw.

The wonder of these airplanes was that huge, strong structures were made up of small sticks.

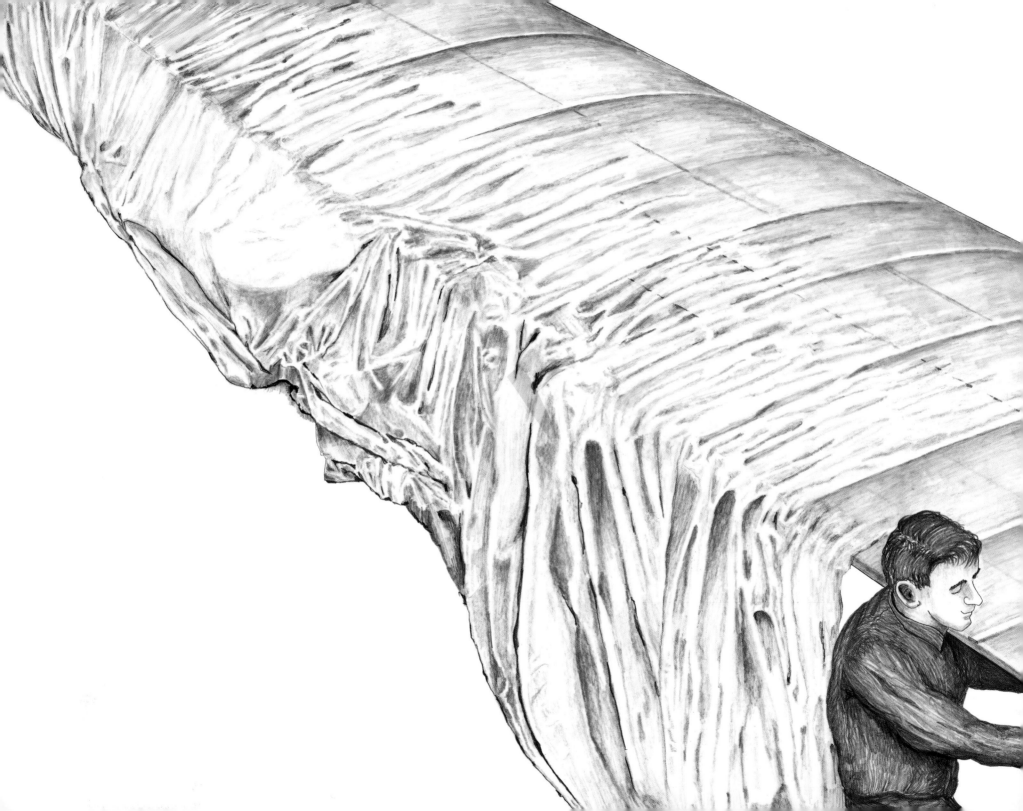

The wings and fuselage were covered with cotton or, sometimes, linen. Narrow lengths of fabric were machine sewn together into pieces big enough to cover a wing panel.

After the fabric had been stretched smooth and tight over the wing and stitched together by hand, the whole wing was sprayed with water. As the cloth dried it shrank and became taut, drum tight. Finally, the wing was brushed with five or six coats of dope, which made it waterproof and airtight (and smelled terrible).

The wonder of it all! Here in this little village, surrounded by miles and miles of small farms, was the only factory in all of America that could mass-produce airplanes—and lots of them. Mr. Curtiss had brought together in this out-of-the-way place some of the best aeronautical engineers in the world. And he began turning out Jennys by the hundreds, and then thousands.

Eventually, Curtiss had to move the plant up to Buffalo, New York. There just weren't enough workers here in Hammondsport. But they continued to make the motors here.

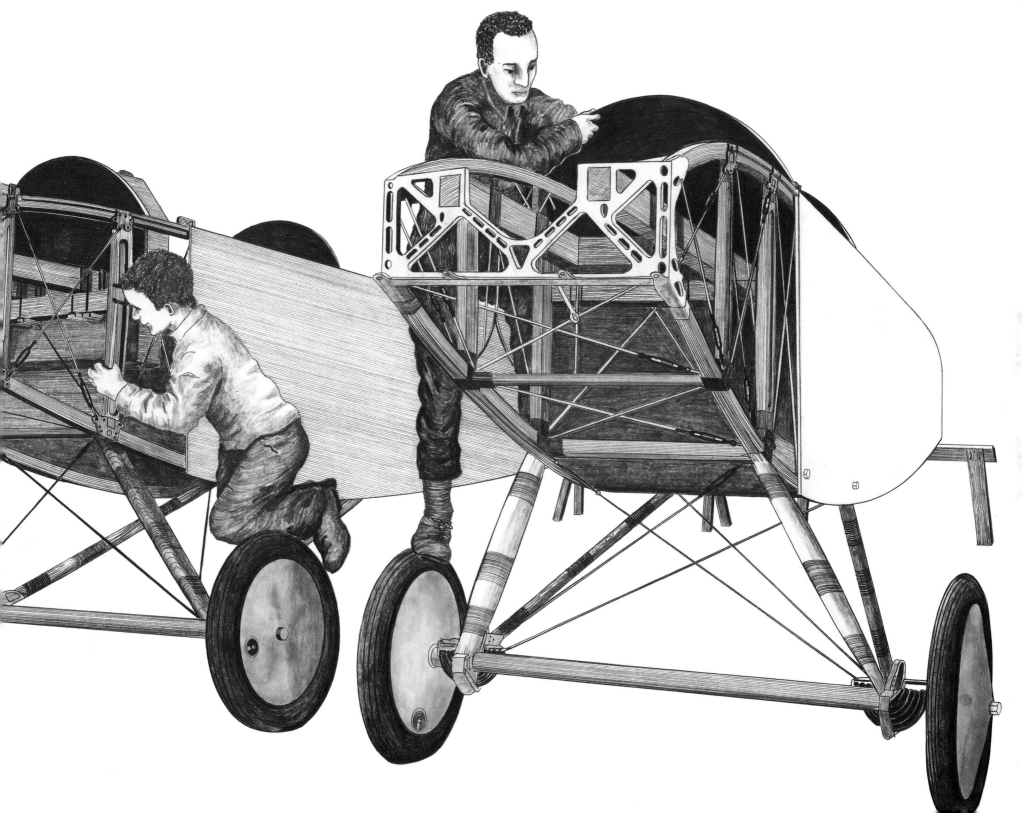

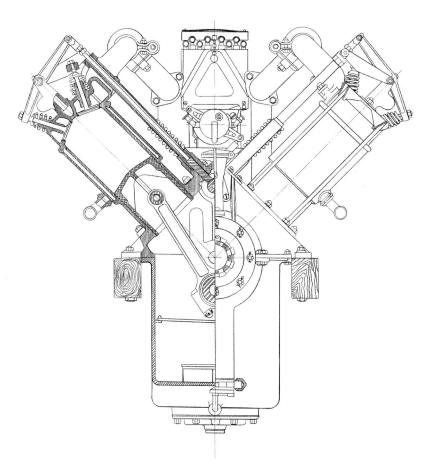

The heart of the Jenny was her OX-5, V-8 engine. Airplane engines must be lightweight as well as powerful. New metals were being introduced to make strong but light engine parts. Pistons and the crankcase were made of aluminum. The water jackets around the cylinders were made of monel metal, a corrosion-resistant alloy. The cylinders were cast iron which was heavy, but still the best wearing metal.

The first aircraft engines were air cooled and could only run a short time before overheating, so the OX-5 was water cooled.

When Mom graduated from high school, she got her
first job at the plant assembling cylinder heads, installing the exhaust and intake
valves. There she was, just sixteen years old, building airplane engines!

During the First World War years, over three thousand employees worked day and night in Hammondsport, machining and assembling OX-5s. All those new folks and their families came to a town of maybe a thousand people, and many of them lived in tents until Mr. Curtiss could get some housing built. What a hubbub. You'd see British Army officers walking smartly through Park Square in full uniform—in little Hammondsport! And there was always the distant roar of the engines being bench tested.

Before the war ended in 1918, the Curtiss plant in Buffalo had manufactured some ten thousand airplanes. The plant's best week's record was 112 airplanes.

Besides Jennys, the "shop," as Curtiss always referred to his plants, was turning out giant NC-4 flying boats—NC standing for Navy Curtiss. Of course, they were called Nancys.

*The children listened with wonder. What an amazing person their great-grandmother had been! And then they turned to the last page of the album. A different young woman in a different flying suit stood proudly by a different plane. Who was she?*

**W**ell, that is me. I guess I just inherited my mother's love of flying. She took me up a lot when I was a youngster, let me take the dual controls. I actually flew a Jenny once myself.

You see, your great-grandmother's generation had a war to fight, and so did mine, World War Two. During that war, American workers built nearly three hundred thousand airplanes. Those planes had to be flown from the factories to air bases all over the country, and from one air base to another. The men were needed to fly combat missions, so I became a WASP, a Women's Airforce Service Pilot. And I flew some pretty hot fighter planes—P-51 Mustangs and P-47 Thunderbolts.

It was fun but it sure could be exhausting. I once flew an AT-6 trainer from Long Beach, California, to Pensacola, Florida, with refueling stops all along the way. After a day's layover I flew a fighter from Pensacola up to Fort Wayne, Indiana, and the next day I was off to Seattle, Washington, as copilot on a C-47 transport plane.

Boy oh boy oh boy. I sure did love to fly.

*Flying High*

*June 1943*

## Acknowledgments

Only the author's name appears on the cover, but *Jenny* represents the enthusiasm and generosity of many people, especially Kirk House and Chris Geiselmann and their staff who welcomed me to the Glenn Curtiss Museum, guided me through the archives and photo collection, and answered my endless questions. Kirk showed me Glenn Curtiss's Hammondsport, a beautiful little town that I imagine remains much as it was when "the fastest man in the world" was building bicycles and motorcycles, starting up "the shop," and experimenting with flying boats on Lake Keuka.

Norm Brush, Chuck Clark, Jack Farmer, Deke Johnson, and Art Wilder, expert volunteer aircraft builders all, invited me into the museum's restoration shop and put me to work helping cover a wing with yards and yards of cotton.

For an understanding of the construction and flying of early aircraft, I turned often to my aviation and aerodynamics consultants, John Hulls, who may have spent more of his life in the air than on the ground, and Horace Irwin, who began his career just before World War Two designing experimental Navy aircraft and retired after working on Thor ballistic missiles.

And thanks also to Darcie Plocher, Brunel and Piper Odegaard, Marion Dusoir Ennes, Jimmy Hankel, and Irv Rosenberg.

Photographs of Katherine Stinson are courtesy of the Glenn Curtiss Museum. Photographs of Jane Baldwin Severy, WASP, are courtesy of her daughter, Nancy Severy. The JN dimensioned general arrangements drawings are the work of Joseph Nieto.

## A Note on the Type

*Jenny* was set in Gill Sans, designed in 1927-8 by the artist-craftsman, Eric Gill, considered by many to be to be the most creative English artist of his generation. Gill was a sculptor and stonecarver, the architect of a beautiful church, an illustrator whose wood engravings appeared in over a hundred books, and designer of eleven typefaces.

Gill Sans was created as an example of what Eric Gill called a "typography of industrialism"—letters to be absolutely legible, clear, and unfussy. His intent was to design a letter that could be drawn by anyone with a ruler and compass, that spoke of "the power of industrialism and the humanity of craftsmanship."

In 1932, Gill himself painted the nameplate for the famous steam locomotive, *Flying Scotsman,* for which he was treated to a high-speed ride in the cab. Gill Sans was adopted as the standard typeface for signs, timetables, and advertising for the London and Northeastern Railway, and is still used today whenever a simple, modern statement is to be made.